APR 1 7 2017

DISCARDED BY
Capital Area District Library

I want to be happy

For my children, Josh & Robbie.

I want to be happy

HOW TO LIVE A HAPPY LIFE

— BY —

Harriet Griffey

hardie grant books

Contents

How happy are you?

Happiness: a mental or emotional state of wellbeing defined by positive or pleasant emotions, ranging from contentment to intense joy.

The pursuit of happiness might be listed, optimistically perhaps, in the US Declaration of Independence, but achieving happiness is something else. The fact that it is seen as something to be actively pursued and, potentially, achieved, makes happiness seem like a box to be ticked, a state of mind to be aimed for above all else.

We can view happiness in at least three ways – as a hedonic state, as a cognitive state, or as a general life philosophy. Happiness, then, can refer to a way of thinking, such as being optimistic; a way of feeling joy, pleasure, relief, or gratitude; or simply a way of being.

NANCY ETCOFF, PHD, PSYCHOLOGIST & COGNITIVE RESEARCHER

Whether you call it subjective wellbeing or positive psychology, much attention has been paid to the subject of happiness in recent years. This new focus has included the publication of a *World Happiness Report* by the United Nations in 2012, 2013 and 2015. Compiled by psychologists, economists, health experts and public-policy advisers, the report reviewed the world's state of happiness and suggested that national governments should pay more attention to happiness, for the benefit of all.

Why? Because happy people are healthier, more productive and cause fewer problems in society, which – if only from an economic point of view – has to be a good thing.

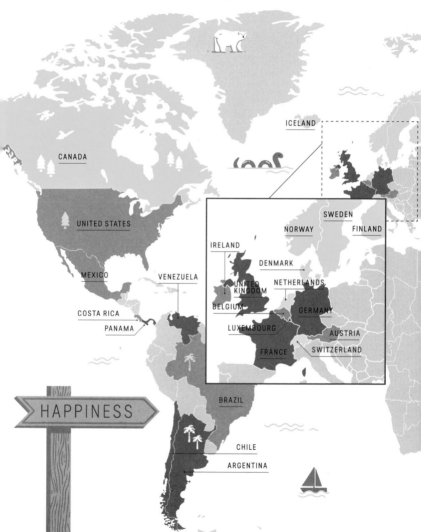

CANADA

UNITED STATES

MEXICO

VENEZUELA

COSTA RICA

PANAMA

BRAZIL

CHILE

ARGENTINA

HAPPINESS

ICELAND

IRELAND

UNITED KINGDOM

BELGIUM

LUXEMBOURG

FRANCE

NORWAY

SWEDEN

FINLAND

DENMARK

NETHERLANDS

GERMANY

AUSTRIA

SWITZERLAND

10

WORLD HAPPINESS REPORT

The Top 30 countries in 2015

1. Switzerland
2. Iceland
3. Denmark
4. Norway
5. Canada
6. Finland
7. Netherlands
8. Sweden
9. New Zealand
10. Australia

11. Israel
12. Costa Rica
13. Austria
14. Mexico
15. United States
16. Brazil
17. Luxembourg
18. Ireland
19. Belgium
20. United Arab Emirates

21. United Kingdom
22. Oman
23. Venezuela
24. Singapore
25. Panama
26. Germany
27. Chile
28. Qatar
29. France
30. Argentina

World Happiness Report criteria is measured in terms of:

- GDP per capita
- Social support
- Healthy life expectancy
- Freedom to make life choices

- Generosity
- Perceptions of corruption
- Positive effect (mood)
- Negative effect (mood)

SINGAPORE

ISRAEL

QATAR

UNITED ARAB EMIRATES

OMAN

AUSTRALIA

NEW ZEALAND

PERMA

It's fascinating to see how different countries can be ranked according to these criteria, and there are several surprises along the way – why, for instance, are the French so much less happy than the Israelis? Scientists have developed different ways to try to measure and assess what makes us happy by looking at a range of very diverse factors such as meaning, resilience, engagement, emotions and accomplishment. American psychologist and acknowledged expert on authentic happiness Dr Martin Seligman is one of the best-known researchers on the subject. He came up with the acronym PERMA, which identifies the five core elements of psychological wellbeing. These elements, according to Dr Seligman, provide us with a scientific model of happiness.

P - POSITIVE EMOTIONS

E - ENGAGEMENT

R - RELATIONSHIPS

M - MEANING

A - ACCOMPLISHMENTS

These elements are clearly pretty self-explanatory, and this framework is a good place to start. However, it's important to remember that even when we have a set of established criteria against which we can try to measure happiness, everyone is different. This framework simply provides a guide towards the steps you can take if you feel that you could be a whole lot happier.

Small steps, big change

When it comes down to it, happiness is all about how you feel, what causes you to feel that way and the realisation that you can make changes, even very small ones, that will make a really big difference. Most people will admit they want to feel happier in some way but until they know what specific action to take, this can feel like all too vague an aspiration. Why not start by identifying what your greatest and most significant sources of happiness and unhappiness are at this moment in time? From this starting point, try and work out what the changes are that might improve how you feel and, just as importantly, how you would go about making those changes.

Happiness quiz

It's not only what we experience in life, but how we feel about those experiences, that will influence whether or not we feel happy. The first crucial step is to work out where you stand right now in terms of happiness. Take this short quiz to get a better picture of your starting point.

› **How do you feel about your life overall at this moment?**
A Optimistic.
B Dissatisfied.
C Frustrated.
D Sad.

› **When you look back on your work achievements, do you feel:**
A Thrilled.
B Pleased at how things have turned out.
C Frustrated. You believe you could have done better.
D Disappointed.

› **How often do you do something just for fun?**
A Every day.
B Every week.
C Once in a blue moon.
D Never.

› **How often do you exercise?**
A Every day.
B Every week.
C Once in a blue moon.
D Never.

› **How many of your friends do you think would happily help you out in a crisis?**
A All my friends.
B About a dozen.
C Just one or two.
D None.

› **How do you sleep?**
A Very well – eight hours a night on average.
B Usually well, but it can depend on what's going on.
C Not too badly, but often wake in the night.
D Very badly – insomnia is always a problem.

> **Do you follow the news every day?**

A Not often, unless there's a big story I am following.
B I check the headlines online in the morning.
C I try to watch the evening news most days.
D I'm a news junkie, following it online, in print and on the radio and television.

> **When you woke this morning, did you feel:**

A Delighted it was time to get up.
B Neutral – neither one thing nor another.
C Apprehensive.
D Despondent.

> **How often do you socialise with friends?**

A Every day.
B Every week.
C Once in a blue moon.
D Never.

> **How do you rate your general health?**

A Excellent.
B Not bad.
C Poor.
D Terrible.

> **Do you have positive memories of your childhood?**

A Yes, it was a happy time.
B Yes, it was good.
C Not really. It was OK, but now is better.
D It was very difficult.

> **If you receive a piece of bad or dispiriting news, how long does it take you to bounce back?**

A Not long, if I can talk it through with someone close.
B A short while, depending on what else is going on.
C A few days. I tend to brood over things.
D Ages. I obsessively go over and over it in my head.

Score your answers

A = 4 points / B = 3 points / C = 2 points / D = 1 point

Score between 48 and 36 points
You're pretty optimistic about life and resilient when it comes to the normal run of ups and downs. You probably already do a variety of things you find rewarding and which help to reinforce your positive outlook on life, and you have a good network of support for when things might be difficult.

Score between 35 and 24 points
You are reasonably content although you may be more influenced by external circumstances than you'd like, and would benefit from introducing new opportunities to enrich your daily life and support networks. This, in turn, will help you build greater resilience and manage the bad times better.

Score between 23 and 12 points
This may be a good time to take a look at how you live your life and whether you are doing enough to balance the negative with the positive. You may need to look closely at your relationships and the work you are doing, and explore whether either of these are causing stress and stopping you from feeling happy. Are you doing enough exercise, getting enough sleep and eating properly? If not, you may want to think about consulting a health professional or seeking some sort of therapy to help you get back on the happiness track.

The happiness gene
– does it exist?

There's no doubt that some people seem to be much happier than others. They appear to always see the best in life and manage its adversities with good humour and, in turn, life seems to work out well for them.

Some people, it appears, have the happiness gene.

Back in 2011, behavioural economists at the London School of Economics asked more than 2,500 people how satisfied they were with their lives while also analysing their DNA for the 'happiness' gene.

The happiness gene, called 5-HTT, is responsible for how well nerve cells manage to distribute serotonin, a chemical produced by the brain that helps enhance a positive mood. People with low levels of serotonin, nicknamed the 'happiness drug', have been found to be more prone to depression. The very premise of a group of antidepressants called *selective serotonin re-uptake inhibitors*, or SSRIs (see page 22), is that they keep more serotonin circulating in the brain, alleviating symptoms of depression, including unhappiness.

> **Of course, our wellbeing isn't determined by this one gene - other genes and, especially, experience throughout the course of life will continue to explain the majority of variation in individual happiness. But this finding helps to explain why we each have a unique baseline level of happiness and why some people tend to be naturally happier than others, and that's in no small part due to our individual genetic make-up.**
>
> *Jan-Emmanuel De Neve, lead researcher*

Does it matter?

But what came first? A genetic predisposition for happiness or a happy life itself? Are those who have the 5-HTT gene happy because of it, or in spite of it? And if the former is true, what does that mean about the latter? Can you be happy if you don't have the happy gene? In other words, is happiness a cause or an effect of circumstance and, if the former, can we really have any influence over it? Could we, in fact, choose to be happy and take steps towards this possibility, actively living life in a way that encourages greater personal happiness, even if we are not by nature or nurture predisposed to it?

> **Most of us are just about as happy as we make up our minds to be.** *William Adams*

What the research shows

The truth is, happiness is not, however much we might like it to be,
an automatic default position. In fact, our more natural inclination is
towards pessimism. Why is this? It turns out that in the past, anticipating
the worst, being hyper-vigilant and generally (understandably) anxious
about being picked off by a prehistoric predator, was a much more helpful
survival mechanism than contentment. Today, however, when our physical
survival is seldom at risk, this natural inclination towards negativity can be
less than helpful in the pursuit of happiness.

Happiness hormones

We may be pessimistic by nature, but we do have good resources to help
boost our mood that, in turn, can help to create a happier state of mind. The
four musketeers, in terms of feel-good hormones, are endorphins, serotonin,
dopamine and oxytocin, which all work in slightly different ways.

› *Endorphins*

Endorphins – or endogenous opioid neuropeptides – are produced by the pituitary gland and central nervous system in response to physical stress and pain. Similar in chemical composition to morphine, endorphins act as a natural painkiller and sedative by activating opioid receptors in the brain. Released during exercise, they trigger positive feelings and can create a natural 'high'. To some extent, they are also produced as a result of emotional stress and pain – to the body, pain is pain; it makes little distinction between whether the pain is emotional or physical.

› *Serotonin*

Serotonin is another feel-good neurotransmitter produced not only in the brain but also in the gut. It helps in the regulation of mood, sexual desire, sleep, appetite, memory and learning. A deficit in serotonin, or in the brain's ability to access it, has been linked with depression. This is why the group of drugs known as SSRIs (selective serotonin reuptake inhibitors) were developed to help treat depression.

› *Dopamine*

Dopamine is a complicated neurotransmitter. It is a key area of scientific interest because it activates the pleasure centre of the brain. When we are expecting something pleasurable to happen, the brain will actually start producing more dopamine. The advantage of this is that this chemical can help motivate us towards doing something that results in this pleasure and reward. So, on one level, the release of dopamine can motivate us to do some work, for example, where the reward is a sense of accomplishment and pride when the work is completed. But in another, less positive way, the release of this feel-good hormone also lies at the heart of the pleasure in, say, gambling or other forms of risk-taking, where the rewards are unpredictable.

Dopamine is also the hormone generated when we 'fall in love', and the pleasure centre of the brain becomes highly activated, allowing us consciously to tap into it. This can motivate our actions towards the goal of feeling better about life, but the downside is that dopamine is also highly addictive, and so lies at the heart of many addictions – whether to love, or slot machines.

› *Oxytocin*

This hormone promotes optimistic feelings, builds self-esteem and trust and is really easy to produce because all you have to do is hug someone. Even just thinking loving and positive thoughts about someone you cherish works, too. Oxytocin release also occurs between mother and baby during breastfeeding to promote bonding, and during sexual intimacy and orgasm to do the same, leading to feelings of security and closeness and earning it the nickname 'the love hormone'. It's what makes us able to empathise with, trust and love one another, which means that the more we can do to create it and spread it around, the happier we could be. So go on, hug someone today. You – and they – will feel happier for it.

Smile more

Positive emotions have a universal signal – the smile – and one that involves not just the mouth, but also a crinkling around the eyes. This is known as the 'Duchenne smile' after the French neurologist Guillaume Duchenne. He identified the use of both the zygomatic major muscle (that lifts the corners of the mouth) and the orbicularis oculi muscle (that raises the cheeks and makes the skin around the eyes crinkle). The interesting thing is that the actual process of moving our facial muscles into a smile increases feelings of positivity: the facial muscles, in smile pose, signal to the brain that we're feeling happy and this improves our overall mood. This positive feedback loop also releases those feel-good endorphins when we smile, so that's another reason why it's worth smiling as often as you can.

> **We shall never know all the good that a simple smile can do.** *Mother Teresa*

Certainly, if someone smiles at us, we almost automatically tend to smile back. This is one small example of how happiness and positivity can actually be passed on through social contact. Nicholas Christakis, Director of the Human Nature Lab at Harvard Medical School, who has researched this phenomenon, discovered that happiness can actually 'rub off' on the people around you. Having a happy friend living within a mile of you actually increases the probability of you being happier, too.

Babies and children smile more often than adults – around 400 times a day. Happy people tend to smile between 40–50 times a day, while, on average, most people smile only around 20 times a day.

Take a walk

Biophilia – a love of, and happy response to, the natural world – has been shown to have a very positive effect on us. Nature, and spending time in natural surroundings, is very restorative to our mood.

Gregory Bratman, from Stanford University, found that a 90-minute walk through a leafy, quiet, park-like environment had a soothing effect on the prefrontal cortex of the brain, and was helpful in reducing the sort of brooding, circular thinking that can predispose us towards anxiety and depression. It also seemed to make those who volunteered for the study happier and more attentive afterwards.

While we need more research to find out exactly why this happens, and which aspects of the natural environment are helpful for increasing happiness, these findings support other work that shows similar positive effects. Even a picture of a beautiful, natural view or fresh plants and flowers in our offices or homes can, it turns out, help lift our mood.

Take a walk outside – it will serve you far more than pacing around in your mind.

RASHEED OGUNLARU

Challenging negative thoughts

You know that negative and persistent voice in your head? That inner critic that can tear you down faster than anyone else you know? Listening to this voice is very unhelpful and self-defeating. *Why are you so mean to yourself?!* Learning to challenge an automatic negative thought pattern, shift that perspective and counter that inner voice can go a long way towards helping you feel much happier.

It's actually quite straightforward to challenge these negative thoughts, but it will take some dedicated practice. This is the process that lies at the heart of cognitive behavioural therapy (CBT), which is all about how changing your thoughts (cognition) helps change how you feel about things and, as a consequence, has a positive effect on how you respond.

My life has been filled with terrible misfortunes, most of which have never happened. *Mark Twain*

When you catch yourself thinking negatively, stop and consider whether what you think is really true or just an imagined, worst-case scenario.

Where's the actual evidence for what you're thinking? Use your first reaction as a spur to reassess what might be getting in the way of letting you see what the reality is. This isn't woolly-brained magical thinking, just an objective look at what the reality of a situation is, without that critical voice in your head telling you otherwise.

The aim here is to use your thinking brain, rather than your feelings, to assess and manage those negative thoughts that are affecting how you feel: to respond rather than react, by thinking differently about a situation.

Is it really true?

Start by testing the reality of what you're thinking. What is the actual *evidence* for it? Check, too, whether or not you're jumping to conclusions that could be unhelpfully negative or self-sabotaging. Our default position is often to see the negative or the worst of a situation and so it takes a deliberate and conscious effort to think differently. One immediate step is to keep things in perspective and, rather than automatically assuming the worst, consider instead, will this really matter in a year's time? Or in a week, a day, or even an hour's time?

Reinforce the positive, not the negative

If the voice in your head is using very emphatic language, for example, 'I *hate* Mondays', it automatically reinforces the idea that Mondays are something to be hated. You can't change the fact that Monday comes along every week, but you can change the way you think about it and, at the very least, stop saying you hate it. You could even find something good to like about it. Maybe book a fun exercise class or do something you actively enjoy on a Monday, so that you have something to look forward to. That way, you could actively begin to *like* Mondays and change not just the voice in your head but the way you think about the start of the working week. Once you've learnt this trick with Mondays, you can use it elsewhere until it becomes a habit.

You can't imagine just how much believing in negative thoughts is affecting your life... until you stop.

CHARLES GLASSMAN

Let go of certainty. The opposite isn't uncertainty. It's openness, curiosity and a willingness to embrace paradox, rather than choose upsides. The ultimate challenge is to accept ourselves exactly as we are, but never stop trying to learn and grow. *Tony Schwartz*, The Energy Project

Be specific

If you have a tendency towards making universal rather than specific statements about life, it's easy to become overwhelmed and feel stuck with a self-fulfilling prophecy. For example, if you say, 'I'm hopeless at relationships', this is unhelpful. First of all, it can't actually be true (*all* relationships, really?) and actually it is so unspecific it gives you no clue as to what you might be able to do to change the feeling that you're hopeless. If, however, you think, 'I am shy around people, which makes getting close to someone difficult', then you can look at how it might be possible to become less shy – and that would eventually help make forming a relationship easier. Once you have something specific to work with, change can quickly occur.

Positive reframing

Take a look at the situation that's getting you down – whether it's a deadline for a piece of work, a tricky conversation you need to have, or a goal you want to set yourself – and then think about turning it into something positive. Thinking of it as a challenge you can overcome, instead of a problem that you can't solve, immediately makes it more positive. Reframing it in this way enables you to take a different, more positive standpoint. This may turn out to be the spur you need for a more positive attitude, too, which can only be a good thing if it lifts your mood and makes you happier.

I've always believed that you can think positive just as well as you can think negative.

JAMES A. BALDWIN

Ventilating

Letting some air in – ventilating a situation – involves being able to talk through a problem or a feeling that's troubling you. Finding the words to do so isn't always easy. Identifying exactly what a feeling is – hurt, sadness, guilt, shame – might not be easy either. Sometimes we can confuse pain with anger, for example. Talking to a trusted friend who listens without judgement can enable us to allow light and air into a situation, which helps ventilate it. Through this process, it can be easier to work out what is the root cause of this unhappiness. That, in turn, can help clarify what steps you can take to help alleviate it.

Seeking advice

Some feelings and situations that directly get in the way of feeling happy can be helped through seeking advice. We can't be experts in everything, including some aspects of ourselves, which is why seeking advice can be so helpful. The clue here is to be specific, to find someone who can help identify what the solution to a problem might be, rather than someone with whom you just go over and over a problem. This is when a trained counsellor or therapist can be helpful (see pages 127–9).

Everything negative – pressure, challenges – is all an opportunity for me to rise. *Kobe Bryant, US basketball legend*

Learn the lessons of the past – & let them go

The first recipe for happiness is: avoid too lengthy meditation on the past. *André Maurois*

A wise person once said, a mistake is just something you did that yielded a result you didn't want. There is no judgement in this description of a mistake and the only error would be to make the same mistake twice. Indeed, we may even say to ourselves, 'I won't make that mistake again.'

Mistakes are a learning opportunity rather than a statement of failure; and many lessons can be learnt in this way if we are open to them.

Experience is the name everyone gives to their mistakes.
Oscar Wilde

Ask for feedback

This can take courage, but it can be a helpful way to see how what you did, didn't work out for you. Sometimes what we do is so flooded by emotion that, in the words of a familiar cliché, it's difficult to see the wood for the trees. An objective, external point of view from someone you trust can be extremely helpful in taking a step towards change and greater happiness.

Make peace with your past

What has happened in the past can impact on the present. If your experiences have been happy and good, this is positive, of course, but where there are unhappy memories or unfinished business, it's good to make your peace with this aspect of your history in order to move on.

Travel light

Let go of what no longer serves you and travel light. Forgive those who have hurt you in the past and move on. Declutter your life of the people and situations that no longer bring pleasure or happiness and clear out that precious space to allow for new possibilities and opportunities.

Each of us has a finite reservoir of energy in any given day. Whatever amount of energy we spend obsessing about missteps we have made, decisions that do not go our way or the belief we have been treated unfairly, is energy no longer available to add value in the world.
Tony Schwartz, The Energy Project

Write a journal

Writing a narrative, your version of events, about what happened and what you learnt from it can help you come to terms with the past, so keeping a daily journal can help the process. Alternatively, if you feel you have become stuck and need some help in resolving how you feel, consider some short-term work with a therapist or counsellor, which will help to create the space to allow you to change your thinking about the past, so that you can feel happier in the present and when thinking about your future.

> **If I'm stuck with my past, giving it purpose feels meaningful to me.**
> *Monica Lewinsky*

Let it go

If this is hard for you there are a number of things that you can do to gain a sense of closure. It may be that writing a letter to someone, even if you never send it, will help you make your peace with what has happened and let it go. It may be that making amends in some way, or saying a goodbye, or clearing out items that keep you connected to an unhappy time, will be an important step in letting go. Don't expect what you do to yield an overnight change, but do make letting go a priority as the end result – closure – will create the space for happier times once any preoccupation with unfinished business is relieved or has gone.

PAST

R is for resilience

Resilience describes our ability to bounce back from bad experiences and tough situations and to recover quickly from difficulties or setbacks. It has become something of a buzzword these days, especially when talking about our capacity for happiness. The good news is that resilience is something that we can consciously foster and develop at any age.

One of the key features of resilient people is that they feel that they have some influence or control over events, and focus on that rather than adopting a victim mentality and constantly asking, 'Why *me*?' They don't become victims of helplessness. So while we can't always predict or control what life will throw at us, we always, always have a choice in how we respond, which then gives us a sense of control.

Everyone experiences tough times; it is a measure of your determination and dedication how you deal with them and how you can come through them. *Lakshmi Mittal*

It's possible to develop resilience to life's adversities at any age, although with the help of supportive adults most people have learnt these skills in response to managing and overcoming difficulties in childhood. In fact, a childhood without challenges can make resilience in adulthood less likely; but whether these skills are learnt in childhood or at an older age, an environment of loving support makes resilience more possible.

> **Man never made any material as resilient as the human spirit.** *Bernard Williams*

Break it down

Rather than feeling overwhelmed by any setback, keep a sense of perspective and see it in context. Ask yourself, again, will it matter in a day's, a week's, a month's or a year's time? It's not the end of the world, but something that has happened and from which you can move on. There may even be useful lessons to learn from what's happened. Ask for feedback from a trusted friend, mentor or life coach; sometimes our subjective view of a situation is inaccurate and an objective take on events can help us gain a more useful positive perspective.

Ask for help

Along with feeling that we have some control, even if it's only control over how we feel about something difficult we're facing, being able to ask for help when we need it is an important part of bouncing back. Asking for help isn't a sign of weakness, but a measure of your self-value and the expectation that you deserve help when necessary. It also shows that you recognise and value others, and that you believe they have something of value to offer you – which is quite a compliment, when you think about it, and reinforces the bonds of friendship.

Success is not final, failure is not fatal: it is the courage to continue that counts.

WINSTON CHURCHILL

Manage stress

Allowing things to get on top of you and feeling overwhelmed makes everything more difficult. Resilient people know how to recognise these feelings and manage them, either day by day, or when they begin to build up. Ensure you get enough sleep, eat regular, healthy meals and make time for both physical exercise and downtime, all of which are essential for maintaining resilience against stress and ensuring that life is all the happier for it.

BENEFITS OF YOGA

A Harvard Medical School study showed that people who do yoga were more capable of dealing with challenges, which in turn helps build resilience. Practising yoga poses to build strength and endurance, and holding the poses while focusing on the breath, helps build your ability to meet a challenge while staying calm and determined.

Happiness does not depend on outward things, but on the way we see them.

LEO TOLSTOY

Avoid catastrophising

'We don't make a drama out of a crisis' was a 1980s advertising slogan (thank you, Commercial Union) and there's something to be said for making this your mantra. Although something awful may have happened to you, chances are it's not the end of the world. Try to think of an alternative or more positive outcome. And, for future events, don't waste time worrying about what could have happened – it's futile and it saps energy that could be put to better use.

Work, challenge, balance & purpose

Work gives you meaning and purpose and life is empty without it. *Stephen Hawking, British physicist*

How do you see the work you do? Is it just a job, or a career or vocation? And how far do the hours you spend doing it make you happy? Is it a means to an end, or an end in itself? Whether you are in paid work, volunteering or still a student, does the work you are doing make you happy?

Along with earning the money we need to finance ourselves, work also provides us with self-definition, identity and self-realisation. It should enable us to use our talents, follow our interests and, in many cases, make a difference not only to our own lives but to those of other people, too. Many people say that in their working life they want to 'make a difference' and want their work to embody some aspect of their personal commitment to life, one that makes them happy.

Everyone has been made for some particular work, and the desire for that work has been put in every heart.

RUMI

Identify what motivates you

Financial reward is just one motivator but for most people that, in itself, is seldom enough compensation. The personal satisfaction gained from what we do, the pleasure of working with other people and our sense of achievement and pride when we complete a task also count for a lot. If this is missing, it's hard to feel happy about going to work each day.

Dr Amy Wrzesniewski, from Yale University's School of Management, concluded that people find positive meaning in work through the work itself, through the contribution they believe it makes to the greater good, through their interactions and relationships with others, and through the opportunity work provides to challenge oneself. Even simple tasks gain meaning when they are connected to personal goals and values.

Do what you can, with what you have, where you are.
Theodore Roosevelt

A study from Keio University in Japan of 6,500 people found that a three-day working week is the best way to ensure employees are productive, once they turn 40. The study found that part-time work is the perfect balance between brain stimulation and stress: people who worked 25 hours a week got the best scores in a number of cognitive performance tests involving words and numbers.

Work/life balance

In a search for a happy working life, it's worth paying attention to your work/life balance. Inevitably there are times when we have to work extensively, even excessively, for short periods of time to complete a project, meet a schedule's demands, hit a deadline, but it's very important to balance this with time out to recharge and refuel. This has become an increasing problem since online technology makes us accessible any time, anywhere; so it's important to monitor its use and turn it off when we can. It's impossible to deliver consistently and to capacity if we hit burnout, which can lead to the sort of physical and emotional stress that predisposes us towards anxiety and depression. This can be an insidious process, building up slowly until it becomes unmanageable, without us really being aware of it, sapping our happiness and enjoyment in life. Monitor the demands made on you through work and be clear about your boundaries.

Choose a job you love and you'll never have to work a day in your life. *Confucius*

The meaning of joy

Joy is more complex than simple happiness. It's that warm, fuzzy feeling you get when you hear your child's laughter, embrace your sweetheart or cuddle a puppy. It's that glorious sunrise shared with another. 'Joy is all about our connection to others,' says George Vaillant, a Harvard Medical School professor who has studied positive emotions. Joy is described as a subconscious, almost physical feeling that appears to stem from the brain's limbic system, which affects how we feel, including feelings of pleasure.

Do anything, but let it produce joy. *Walt Whitman, poet*

As joy is so akin to happiness, and contributes to it, it's as well to consider ways you can increase and enhance joy in your own life. Taking steps to do this will significantly improve your mood and enhance your happiness.

Mahatma Gandhi's famous saying, *'Be the change you wish to see in the world'* could easily be rephrased to, *'Be the joy you wish to see in the world'*. Start here, and start now. Look for the joy in the simple pleasures of life and then share them.

Joy does not simply happen to us. You have to choose joy and keep on choosing it.

HENRI NOUWEN

Enjoy the view

Get outside for a part of every day and take joy in the natural environment. Notice the change in the seasons: the first buds of spring, the full leaf of summer, the crisp mornings of autumn, the cosy nights of winter. If you live in a city with a metro, take the bus rather than the subway if you can. Walk whenever possible. On your computer, upload a screensaver of beautiful views of places you know, love, have enjoyed or want to visit.

To be interested in the changing seasons is a happier state of mind than to be hopelessly in love with spring. *George Santayana*

Make plans

Half the fun and enjoyment of any activity lies in the planning and anticipation. Involve your friends. Create and share memorable experiences. Do things that bring you joy to counterbalance those aspects of everyday life that you find more mundane. Play lovely music while you wash up, listen to that classic serial while you drive; do what you can to enhance your enjoyment of life.

Focus on what's good

'My experience is what I agree to attend to,' said psychologist, philosopher and doctor William James (brother of the more famous Henry) and he's right: if you decide to focus on what's good in your life, then that becomes your experience of your life. By exerting a choice, you are effectively choosing to be happier. Make a conscious effort to see the positive, rather than the negative, in life – and celebrate it.

Once you're caught in the mousetrap, why not eat the cheese? *John Alejandro King*

Sometimes your joy is the source of your smile, but sometimes your smile can be the source of your joy.

THICH NHAT HANH

Mix with happy people

The Framingham Heart Study, carried out between 1983 and 2003 in Massachusetts, found that happy people tend to be connected to one another – so, no surprise there. What was surprising was that the study also found that the clusters of happy and unhappy people in the study's network were significantly larger than expected by chance and that a person's happiness is directly associated with their proximity to happy people, something the researchers called 'emotional contagion'.

ODE TO JOY

In the summer of 1785, the German poet, playwright and historian Friedrich Schiller wrote his famous 'Ode to Joy', which inspired the final movement of Beethoven's Ninth Symphony, also known as the Choral Symphony. This, in turn, was adopted in 1972 by the Council of Europe and, subsequently, the European Union, to become its anthem. It's a stirring, momentous piece of joyous music, which can't fail to lift your heart and soul.

JOMO

Sometimes we overextend ourselves for Fear of Missing Out or FOMO. We accept every invitation and do too much because we don't want to miss out on anything. Discover, instead, the Joy of Missing Out or JOMO – that delicious feeling that you've got time on your hands, a unexpected gap in your schedule with no demands, and the sheer pleasure of the prospect of doing what you want to do, whatever that might be, with joy.

> **Find out where joy resides, and give it a voice far beyond singing. For to miss the joy is to miss all.**
> *Robert Louis Stevenson*

Food & mood

That old adage, *'You are what you eat'*, contains more than a grain of truth. Running on empty does us no favours and food is the fuel on which we thrive. What we eat should support both our bodies and minds for optimal performance, including happiness. You probably already know it's hard to be happy when you're hungry or suffering from low blood-sugar levels.

> **One cannot think well, love well, sleep well, if one has not dined well.** *Virginia Woolf*

Eat regularly

The clue is in its name: breakfast. We break our overnight fast with the first meal of the day. It can make all the difference if we allow time to eat a healthy breakfast that balances carbohydrates for energy with protein; this combination helps avoid the insulin surge that creates feelings of hunger. Slow-release carbs also help here. That old English staple – boiled egg with toast soldiers – is a perfect example, especially if the toast is made from wholemeal or spelt bread. If you want to avoid bread, then eat your egg with some oatcakes. Alternatively, some fruit – an apple or pear – with some cheese (very Scandinavian) gives the same carb–protein combination. Even avocado and bacon on a bagel will set you up well. For even greater slow-release carbs, eat porridge (oatmeal) and sweeten with fruit rather than sugar. Eat a banana, at least, if you can't face anything more – it's the ultimate in fast food! Be inventive, but enjoy breakfast; it will pay dividends in terms of enhancing your mood at the beginning of the day.

Avoid snacking between meals if you can but, if you need a power snack, go for some high-protein fruit and nuts: walnuts, almonds or Brazil nuts are all good and dried apricots are a nutritional powerhouse, complete with iron.

Before bed

If you are prone to mood-zapping early-morning waking, make sure you finish your day with a late-night snack – warm milk with cinnamon, slow-release carbohydrates such as porridge, or some other wholegrain cereal, which will promote sleepiness and sustain you overnight. If it's hunger that's kick-starting your wake-up hormones in the early hours, this should help you sleep longer and so wake up happier.

After a good dinner one can forgive anybody, even one's own relations. *Oscar Wilde*

Keep it natural

Whenever you can, opt for freshly prepared food over processed or 'junk' foods, which tend to be high in fats, sugars, salt and other additives designed to extend their shelf life, not yours! Organic or locally grown fresh fruit and vegetables should form the basis of your diet, balanced with protein, fats and other carbohydrates.

Sugar

Avoid added sugars. These contribute to a lot of 'empty' calories – i.e. calories that provide little else of nutritional value. Our sugar intake has rocketed over the last 100 years from about 5 kg (11 lb) per person a year to 68 kg (150 lb), with all the associated weight gain that implies. A high sugar intake also adversely affects vitamin B metabolism – an important vitamin for supporting the nervous system.

Laughter is brightest in the place where the food is. *Irish proverb*

Water

Keep hydrated. Thirst isn't a particularly good guide and dehydration can affect energy levels and mood, and in some susceptible people make them more prone to headaches. Other drinks contribute, but keep an eye on your caffeine intake – from coffee and also other caffeinated drinks. Caffeine can be overstimulating and make you 'jangly' in excess.

OMEGA-3 ESSENTIAL FATTY ACIDS

Most Westernised diets tend to be low in omega-3 EFAs, not least because our diets tend to be high in omega-6 EFAs from vegetable sources, and these compete against omega-3 EFAs for absorption. Natural sources of omega-3 EFAs come from oily fish such as mackerel, herring, salmon and tuna. Considerable research shows that omega-3 EFAs have a positive and stabilising effect on mood. One study, published by the *Australian and New Zealand Journal of Psychiatry* in March 2008, showed that a gram of omega-3 EFA was as clinically effective in trials as a 20 mg dose of Prozac a day. If you need to supplement, choose a pharmaceutical grade omega-3 EFA product, to provide an adequate source of active ingredient.

But… most of all, enjoy the preparation of a meal, share it with friends and make it a happy experience.

A good cook is like a sorceress who dispenses happiness.

ELSA SCHIAPARELLI

Sleep – how it helps

Sleep is extremely important to happiness and mood. It helps regulate both, keeping us balanced and positive, both of which help us to feel happier. REM (rapid eye movement) sleep, when we dream, is also important because it is during this stage that we process daily events and memories, shifting their storage from short-term to long-term memory. So if sleep goes haywire, insomnia and constant waking can cause (and also be caused by) low mood and depression. It's easy to see how this can become a vicious circle.

> **Sleep, that knits up the ravell'd sleave of care,**
> **The depth of each day's life, sore labour's bath,**
> **Balm of hurt minds, great nature's second course,**
> **Chief nourisher in life's feast.**
> *William Shakespeare, Macbeth (Act II, scene ii)*

This connection between sleep and happiness has been consistently borne out by research. For example, research carried out by neuroscientist

Matthew Walker, based at the University of California, Berkeley, found that while a good night's rest can regulate mood and help you cope with the next day's emotional challenges, sleep deprivation does the opposite by excessively firing up that part of the brain most closely connected to depression, anxiety and other psychiatric disorders. 'It's almost as though, without sleep, the brain had reverted back to more primitive patterns of activity, in that it was unable to put emotional experiences into context and produce controlled, appropriate responses,' says Walker. 'Emotionally, you're not on a level playing field.'

Sleep is the golden chain that ties health and our bodies together. *Thomas Dekker*

It's useful to think of sleep as an important aspect of life and one that has to be cherished and nurtured to protect our wellbeing. Some people are more sensitive to sleep deprivation than others, but for many, chronic lack of sleep can have a profound effect on their happiness – and not without reason. Deep sleep, in particular, helps in mood regulation and so without regular, good sleep we will become moody, irritable and anxious.

In 2014, a poll from Gallup-Healthways in the United States found that 42 per cent of the 7,000 adults surveyed got less than the seven hours sleep a night recommended by the National Sleep Foundation. What the poll also found was that the average wellbeing score for people who reported getting eight hours of sleep a night was 65.7/100, compared with 64.2/100 for those who got seven hours of sleep and 59.4/100 for those who only got six hours of sleep. The scores were based on the participants' answers to questions about their sense of purpose, social relationships, financial lives, community involvement and physical health. Not a huge difference, maybe, but an increase, nevertheless, in the wellbeing score amongst those reporting more sleep.

Early to bed and early to rise makes a man healthy, wealthy and wise.

BENJAMIN FRANKLIN

If lack of sleep is troubling you, then it's important to take steps to get back on track. Bear in mind that when sleep patterns have become seriously disrupted over a long period of time, it is not something that can be resolved overnight. And also remember that sleep is part of your 24-hour day, so what happens throughout the whole day will have an impact on how well you sleep at night.

A good laugh and a long sleep are the best cures in the doctor's book.

IRISH PROVERB

CRISIS MANAGEMENT PLAN

- Avoid all stimulants, such as caffeine, alcohol and nicotine throughout the day.

- Keep regular hours: getting up in the morning and going to bed at roughly the same time each day helps reset your internal clock.

- Take daily exercise – preferably in the daylight to help regulate your internal body clock.

- Avoid all work and excessive physical activity for at least two hours before bed; allow time for the body and mind to relax.

- Don't read from backlit screen devices such as laptops and smartphones in bed, as these overstimulate the brain.

- Have a light snack before sleep: try milky drinks or cereals that contain the sleep-inducing amino acid tryptophan.

- Try a magnesium and vitamin B supplement, drink chamomile tea, or add some lavender essential oil to a bath before bed.

- Have your sleeping area as quiet and dark as possible; darkness aids the brain's secretion of sleep-inducing melatonin. Use earplugs, too.

Exercise – how it also helps

Exercise is the secret weapon of mood enhancement and works in a number of different ways to increase feelings of happiness, not just by taking us out of ourselves but also by creating those mood-enhancing chemicals that lift our spirits. Research also suggests that exercise can actually help ward off depression and anxiety by further enhancing our natural ability to respond to stress. What's more, it takes relatively little regular exercise to make a really big difference to our mood and levels of happiness – fact.

Exercise is really important to me – it's therapeutic. So if I'm ever feeling tense or stressed or like I'm about to have a meltdown, I'll put on my iPod and head to the gym or out on a bike ride.

Michelle Obama, former First Lady

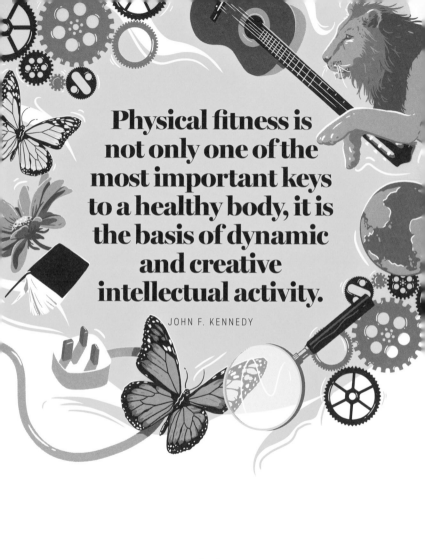

Physical fitness is not only one of the most important keys to a healthy body, it is the basis of dynamic and creative intellectual activity.

JOHN F. KENNEDY

Endorphins

Endorphins (see page 22) are mood-enhancing hormones produced in response to physical exercise. This is useful because endorphins are released in response to physical pain and stress, and also help alleviate emotional pain and stress. (Remember, it doesn't matter much to the body whether the source of pain and stress is physical or emotional.) Endorphins have similar pain-relieving and soothing effects to morphine, and they also increase positive feelings. To this end, regular exercise greatly improves mood, especially if you are feeling low or depressed.

Serotonin

Exercise can also increase brain serotonin (see page 22), even for older adults, suggesting that regular exercise may act as a natural antidepressant and anti-ageing strategy for the brain.

Balance

Exercise also helps to balance the sympathetic nervous system (SNS) with the parasympathetic nervous system (PNS). Why is this important? The SNS is the central nervous system's accelerator. Fired up, the heart pumps faster, breathing rate increases and the muscles are primed for activity – at its extreme, this is the fight-flight-freeze mechanism designed for survival. To counter this effect, we have the PNS, which acts as a brake to the often overactive SNS. The PNS is controlled by the vagus nerve, which runs from the base of the skull past the larynx, down to the heart, diaphragm and organs of the gut, calming them all down. People who exercise regularly show better balance between the SNS and the PNS, so it would seem that the more stimulation it receives, the stronger the PNS becomes and the more balanced our two systems – the SNS and the PNS – are. We need this balance to keep our mood stable.

> **What appears to be happening is that exercise affords the body an opportunity to practise responding to stress, streamlining the communication between the systems involved in the stress response. The less active we become, the more challenged we are in dealing with stress.**
> *J. Kip Matthews, PhD, sport and exercise psychologist*

What else?

It's not just about the physical activity, either. When we take time out to exercise, we often spend time around other people; exercise can be something we do to socialise and that, too, will help lift our mood.

Exercise is often something we do outside, so we gain here by being in full-spectrum light or mood-enhancing sunshine and by being in a natural environment, all of which are also known to lift mood and increase feelings of happiness.

Taking time out to concentrate on physical rather than mental activity can also help stop that process of circular thinking and ruminating on negative thoughts, which only serves to reinforce them and make them more persistent.

An early morning walk is a blessing for the whole day.

HENRY DAVID THOREAU

Choose exercise that you can easily factor into your daily routine – something you could do with other people but also, if necessary, alone. Walking is a good example of this. You can walk every day on your own, but you could also join a walking group to make the activity more sociable and to enable you to tackle longer walks. Yoga can be done in class, but also practised at home. A hardcore workout in the gym or some intensive weight-lifting can be balanced by swimming or t'ai chi. It really doesn't matter what form of regular exercise you choose, it will still improve your general level of happiness. Start gently, but do it regularly and build on it.

Combining mental and physical training has been shown to have a positive effect on mood. Research from the Department of Exercise Science at Rutgers, the State University of New Jersey, with a mixed group (including those with a diagnosis of major depressive disorder), showed good results after only eight weeks of combining two 60-minute sessions a week of focused-attention meditation followed by moderate-intensity aerobic exercise. By doing both, participants showed a reduction in 'ruminative thought processes' and an increase in 'cognitive control processes'. Just one hour, twice a week, over eight weeks showed a 40 per cent reduction in their symptoms.

Rest & relaxation; mindfulness & meditation

Fact: downtime is essential to happiness.

The relentless pace of modern living, with its global, 24/7 work ethic and its do-it-all, have-it-all *NOW!* impulses, often obscures the very real need for downtime. We all need to recharge our batteries and it's impossible to do this when assaulted by constant demands. Downtime is essential for consolidating brain activity and re-energising us.

Without rest and relaxation, neither our bodies nor our brains can function well. We begin to rely more and more on those stress hormones – cortisol and adrenaline – that will keep us going but, in time, insidiously erode our wellbeing. Fuelled by stress hormones, we find that sleep becomes more elusive, and chronic fatigue, which is closely aligned to depression and anxiety, can creep up on the most robust of us. Better then to ensure that adequate downtime is factored into busy schedules, as much a priority as anything else we have to do, in order to preserve our sanity and happiness. It is not a false economy.

Take a rest. A field that is rested gives a beautiful crop. *Ovid*

Balance the brain

We tend to be what is loosely called 'left-brained' in our day-to-day life, as we generally rely on left-brained functions like reading and writing for our work. A more relaxed state allows our right-brain functioning greater capacity. This can be very helpful for creative problem-solving, as well as mood-stabilising, so it's well worth considering using mindfulness and meditation to help balance the brain's activities.

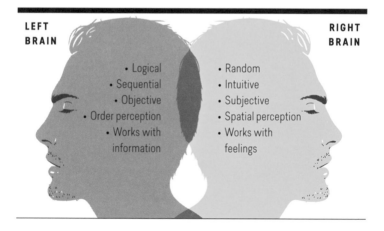

LEFT BRAIN
- Logical
- Sequential
- Objective
- Order perception
- Works with information

RIGHT BRAIN
- Random
- Intuitive
- Subjective
- Spatial perception
- Works with feelings

Reclaim the nap

For a nap to work best, to be restorative rather than compensatory for a poor night's sleep, it should last between 20 and 30 minutes. Any shorter doesn't count as a nap, any longer can mean you hit a deeper sleep phase, making it difficult to resume what you were doing before. There's good evidence to show that taking your foot off the metaphorical gas for some daytime downtime is very effective at restoring energy, mood and concentration, enabling your brain to work much more effectively. No wonder it's become known as 'power napping'.

A nap can also break that cycle of rumination and worry – that habit of going over and over something in your mind. Ineffective worrying is a barrier to happiness and can be a difficult habit to break. This is why taking a break from it by having a nap can restore your good humour and improve feelings of happiness.

Feelings come and go like clouds in a windy sky. Conscious breathing is my anchor.

THICH NHAT HANH

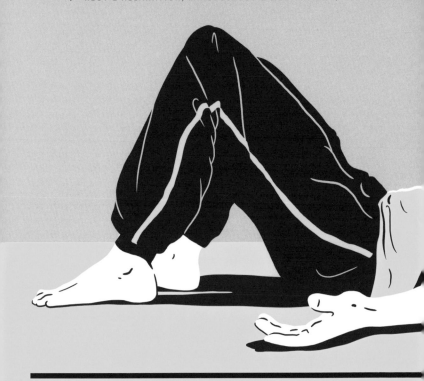

AND BREATHE...

- Lie comfortably on the floor, knees bent, chin tucked in – this is what Alexander Technique teachers call the 'constructive rest position' – or sit upright in a chair, legs uncrossed, feet flat on the floor.
- Consciously relax your neck and drop your shoulders, rest your arms by your sides with your palms turned upwards.
- Breathe slowly and gently in through your nose, into your belly until you feel it gently rise, for a slow count of five.

- Pause, and hold that breath for a count of five, then gently exhale through your mouth for another slow count of five.
- While doing this, try to clear your mind of all other thoughts or, if this is difficult, close your eyes and visualise a pebble dropping into a pool of water and gently sinking, slowly, down.
- Repeat this breathing cycle ten times, then see how your regular breathing adjusts.
- You can also use this breathing technique any time you feel tense or stressed, or as the basis of any meditation practice.

> **If you want to conquer the anxiety of life, live in the moment, live in the breath.** *Amit Ray*

Practise mindfulness and gratitude

Living in the moment is really what mindfulness is all about. It's not about stopping what you are doing so much as taking time to focus fully on and savour what you do – whether that's cooking a meal, writing an essay, talking with a friend, reading your child a story, taking a walk – so you can truly engage and feel rewarded by the experience, rather than resenting the demand on your (precious) time.

When you are mindful, it makes it easier to practise gratitude. Practising gratitude, acknowledging thankfulness for small pleasures, helps reinforce the positive side of life, fuelling a sense of happiness. It's a good habit to cultivate – gratitude for the supply of water with which we can wash our dishes doesn't make doing the washing-up less of a chore, but it does remind us that in washing a dish we have been fortunate enough to be able to enjoy a meal, we have access to food, and the comfort of that.

Meditation

The practice of meditation will make you feel happier, according to research done by psychiatrist Dr Howard Cutler in association with the Dalai Lama, as part of a lifestyle of mindfulness. You can learn meditation alone, or you can find a class, but it does take time and practice to become proficient. It is an active process, not a relaxation technique, and takes conscious effort to focus your attention on the here and now, allowing thoughts to pass without engagement, judgement or analysis. This disengagement from frenetic thought helps restore positivity and calm, releasing tension and allowing happier feelings.

- Create a regular routine – practise twice a day for a minimum of 10 minutes.
- Find a quiet place, where you won't be interrupted.
- Sit in a comfortable, upright position.
- Start with the breathing exercise (pages 76–7).
- Find an external point of focus – some like to focus on a candle flame, a flower or abstract symbol – or an internal point of focus in your mind's eye.
- Use a mantra – this can be a single word or a phrase, repeated, which helps bring you back to a single point of focus.
- One popular Tibetan Buddhist mantra is *'Om mani padme hum'*, which translated means 'Om, jewel of the lotus' and has a nice, reverberating feel to it.
- If alone, the mantra can be said aloud or, if with others, repeated silently.
- The mantra, combined with the focus on your breathing helps to create a meditative state.
- Meditation takes practice, so don't give up if you're not convinced that it's helping straight away.

Meditation is a little drop of perfume that suffuses the day with its grace.

R. D. LAING

Having fun

Relax! Switch off! Have fun! Be happy!

If there was anything more likely to make you disinclined to have fun, being exhorted to do so probably ranks right up there with someone saying, 'Smile: it may never happen!' In spite of this, it's worth pausing to consider how having fun with family, friends, colleagues – and even like-minded strangers you could meet at a sporting event or music concert – can generate happiness.

A stranger's just a friend you haven't met yet. *Marge Simpson*

Create positive experiences

This doesn't need to be momentous, like an adventure holiday or a big party, but can be one of those small daily events that occur through which we can find pleasure. So much of what we have to do, day by day, can be monotonous, mundane and routine but what can help enliven this is how we approach it. So if that daily bus journey to work is grim, consider what might make it more fun: could you talk to a travelling companion, listen to an audiobook or alternate taking the bus with walking to work?

Never put off till tomorrow the fun you can have today.
Aldous Huxley

Have fun with friends

Nurture social relationships, which are key to our happiness, through having fun together. This doesn't mean that you have to accept every invitation that comes your way, but it does mean being open to the possibility that fun can be shared in the context of social relationships. It also means creating those opportunities – connecting with friends, suggesting ideas, making plans – that suit what you want to do, too. Being the instigator of fun times means you get to choose to do what you enjoy and then to make it happen.

I've taken my fun where I've found it. *Rudyard Kipling*

Get curious

You can have fun expressing your curiosity in all sorts of ways, from the way you dress to what you cook, from the books you read to the music you listen to. When something interests you, you can explore it further by taking a class or joining a group of enthusiasts. Curiosity is a way of exploring the world that refreshes you and replenishes your batteries, whether it's curiosity about people or places, art or architecture, the natural world or high tech. Take a photography class, keep a journal, take up drawing, dancing, cooking – anything that expresses your curiosity in a way that's fun and makes you happy.

REMEMBER...
Having fun is an important part of life.
Having fun doesn't have to involve big plans or lots of money.
Having fun can happen spontaneously – be open to it.
Having fun doesn't have to be PERFECT.
Having fun can happen by yourself, with a friend, in a crowd.
Having fun can make you happy.

You can discover more about a person in an hour of play than in a year of conversation.

PLATO

The cure for boredom is curiosity. There is no cure for curiosity.

ELLEN PARR

Relationships
– only connect

Our relationships, with family, friends and loved ones, lie at the very heart of our happiness. There's no way around this. We are social beings programmed to connect with one another, and our ability to form and sustain social relationships goes a long way to ensuring our happiness – protecting our heart, if you like, from damage in both an emotional and physical sense.

   This is because, at its simplest level, in prehistoric times being social and living in social groups afforded us protection and enhanced survival. Our social connections also help support our physical health. Research has shown that feeling loved and nurtured means our bodies function better and stress hormones aren't constantly on red alert: our heart and immune system are stronger, we are less vulnerable to infection and we can focus without the distraction of having to find the support we need. This frees us from anxiety and depression, contributing to our happiness.

Man is by nature a social animal. Anyone who either cannot lead the common life or is so self-sufficient as not to need to, and therefore does not partake of society, is either a beast or a god. *Aristotle*

How we affect others

Thanks to the research of those like psychologist Daniel Goleman, we have a far greater understanding today of what's called social intelligence, and how our moods affect others, and vice versa. We all know how great it feels to be around happy and light-hearted people – it lifts our mood and makes us feel happier, too. So it makes sense not only to spend time with happy people, but also to be like them and to share good feelings around.

A true partner or friend is one who encourages you to look deep inside yourself for the beauty and love you've been seeking. *Thich Nhat Hanh*

Social networking

Connecting with others digitally – online, via text or email, Facebook or instant messenger – just isn't enough. Forming social relationships has to be done in real life. Good though it is to reach out in this way, all the digital connections and friends on Facebook won't compensate. If you want it to yield happiness, social-media socialising should only ever be an adjunct to real-life interaction.

Your friend is your needs answered. He is your field, which you sow with love and reap with thanksgiving. And he is your board and your fireside. For you come to him with your hunger, and you seek him for peace.

KAHLIL GIBRAN

Sharing good times

Sharing time together is a key component of good relationships, and sharing pleasurable and enjoyable times in person – over meals, on walks, on holidays – with other people, family and friends, creates space for the communication on which our relationships can thrive. Only in person can we communicate on all levels and create the sort of empathetic connection that transcends the spoken word.

When relationships go wrong

Even though we may be wired to be social, it's not always easy to do this. But because of the benefits to our happiness it's well worth taking steps to address relationship issues when they occur. And because we are also wired for self-protection, this may mean removing ourselves from relationships that are causing us unhappiness. Better to restore, create or nurture those that do make us happy. In circumstances where this isn't possible, perhaps with family members or work colleagues, then finding strategies to avoid being adversely affected by them (which isn't easy) may be the only option.

The best thing to hold onto in life is each other.

AUDREY HEPBURN

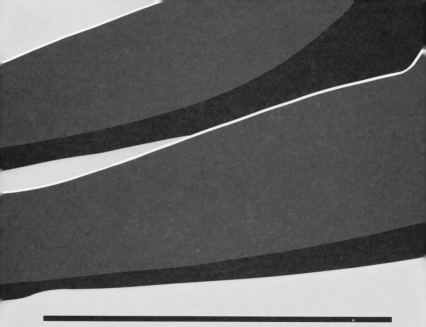

TOP TIPS TO REPAIR FRIENDSHIPS

- **Let the dust settle:** If there's been a difference of opinion, an argument or confrontation, you may need to give it a little time, which creates the opportunity to evaluate what you might lose if you let the friendship go.
- **Reach out:** When you're ready, reach out: be the first to do so, if necessary, and don't leave it too long. Reaching out shows that you care enough about your friend and your friendship with them to do so.
- **Leave your ego out of it:** Sometimes it's all too easy to get caught up with your own ego about what happened. Feeling hurt and defensive can get in the way, so acknowledge those feelings and try to understand the other's point of view with empathy.
- **Say sorry:** There is no shame in apologising, but it has to be meant. An authentic apology is one of the best ways to repair a friendship.
- **Forgive and forget:** If you have been wounded in some way by a friend, but can find a way to forgive them then move on, and forget it. Don't hold a grudge or allude to what happened in the future, or it will taint your friendship.

The importance of love

'All you need is love!' as the Beatles famously sang, and they were not far wrong. We may need food, water and oxygen, too, but in order to really thrive our biological need for love is just as strong.

Love, through its expression in hugs, smiles, kissing and sexual intimacy, promotes the secretion of oxytocin (see page 23), a feel-good hormone produced by both men and women that helps us form loving attachments to others and generally creates feelings of contentment and happiness. It is an antidote to stress hormones, so produces feelings of calm in the body, allowing us to relax and function well.

Each of us can learn the art of nourishing happiness and love. Everything needs food to grow, even love. If we don't know how to nourish our love, it withers. When we feed and support our own happiness, we are nourishing our ability to love. That's why to love means to learn the art of nourishing our happiness. *Thich Nhat Hanh*

Where there is love there is life.

MAHATMA GANDHI

Babies born prematurely who need specialised medical care to survive their early births were found to be much more likely to thrive if they were kept close to their mothers or another caregiver at all times. 'Kangaroo care', as this skin-to-skin care became known, with babies naked apart from a nappy, and held close to the mother's skin, helps babies thrive because they physically tune in to their mother. This proximity helps them regulate their body temperature, heart and breathing rates. It improves oxygen intake and results in more rapid weight gain, better sleep patterns and more rapid brain development, in spite of their prematurity. These babies not only have greater survival rates, but positively thrive through this closeness.

Absence of love makes us unhappy

This may sound obvious, but we can see how beneficial it is to love and be loved by considering what effect emotional pain and unhappiness can have on our emotional and physical wellbeing. One of the benefits of recent developments in neuroscience has been the ability to look at brain activity via functional magnetic resonance imaging (fMRI) – where scientists can actually see which parts of the brain are active under what conditions. For example, using fMRI to scan the brain it's possible to see that the pain of emotional loss and rejection looks a whole lot like the physical pain of, say, breaking your leg. To the brain and the body, pain is pain, whether its source is emotional or physical.

So, even though a broken heart and a broken leg may seem like very different forms of pain, the body experiences it in similar ways. There are good reasons why our brains process pain in this way, because pain is a sign that something is wrong and we need to take action. In evolutionary terms, social isolation makes us vulnerable and puts us at risk, so emotional pain is a signal to form connections that will protect us.

Loving relationships support our happiness and longevity

We may not need the presence of others to protect us physically today, but loneliness is a big risk factor in anxiety, depression and unhappiness. Social connection and love are still crucial for our day-to-day happiness and, it turns out, this can even affect our longevity.

A report by Dan Buettner, published in *National Geographic* magazine in 2005, identified those factors that were linked to longevity in three communities (as diverse as those from Sardinia in Italy, Okinawa in Japan and among Seventh-Day Adventists in California, USA) and found that top of the list were putting family first and keeping socially engaged; the others were regular exercise, eating a plant-based diet and not smoking. Social connection and loving relationships are highly relevant to our happiness and even our health.

We know that people who are having sex after the age of 50, at least twice a week, have about half the rate of mortality than people who aren't getting it.

DAN BUETTNER, NATIONAL GEOGRAPHIC
FELLOW AND BESTSELLING AUTHOR

FIVE WAYS TO NURTURE HAPPY RELATIONSHIPS

- **Presence:** Be there, in person. Turn off any distractions (television, phone, computer) and be there in body and spirit.
- **Time:** Take time, make time for those you love, and expect the same in return.
- **Listen:** Active listening, without distractions or interruptions, can open up good communication.
- **Share:** Find activities that can be enjoyed together: walking, watching sport or a favourite television programme, reading silently together or listening to music. Whatever you can enjoy sharing together, find it and share it.
- **Show affection:** Physically – through a hug, a foot rub or shoulder massage. Connect physically, without words or agenda, regularly. This applies to everyone, from grumpy adolescent boys to elderly grandparents. Everyone needs positive reaffirmation through companionable touch.

Families

Families come in all shapes, sizes and configurations. They can be the source of our greatest joy and happiness, or our greatest frustration and despair. Within our family is where we learn our first lessons about life and, if we're lucky, these lessons will be positive ones and support us throughout our lives. However sentimental we may be about families, there's no such thing as a 'perfect' one; all families are the sum total of their parts, fashioned by those who create them.

All happy families are alike; each unhappy family is unhappy in its own way. *Leo Tolstoy*

Unlike our friends, we don't choose our families; we are born into them. Sometimes we create our own version of a family with those with whom we share much more in terms of values and interests and this is of equal importance to the birth family – sometimes, more so.

The bond that links your true family is not one of blood, but of respect and joy in each other's life. *Richard Bach*

However a family is configured, everyone wants it to be a happy one. Creating happy families requires constant navigation, adjusting our expectations throughout the course of its life, where we go from being a dependent babe to an autonomous adult, via all the stages in between. How we negotiate this depends on the personalities and the dynamics played out between us and, as we change, so do these dynamics.

Researchers have found that a loving family life can be created among any group of people. Long-term studies comparing adopted children to children raised by their biological parents find little difference in the children's feelings on family life, and no difference in their ability to enjoy good relationships with peers. *Dr Linda Neiheiser, psychologist, Kent State University, Ohio*

TIPS FOR HAPPY FAMILY LIFE

- **Eat together:** Routinely sharing a meal together, if not once a day then at least several times a week, creates a relaxed opportunity for communication.

- **Try differently:** Families are organic and subject to change; if one way of doing things isn't working, don't try harder to enforce it but try *differently*. Needs and expectations change over time, even in families; be open to this.

- **Be flexible:** No one is wholly right or wrong when there's a difference of opinion and families should be a safe place to explore and formulate ideas. Respect is as important in a family as anywhere else.

- **Support each other:** When the chips are down, knowing someone is on your side makes all the difference. Show this support in affectionate and practical ways and enable even the youngest members of the family to learn how to do the same.

- **Have fun:** If you want your family to be a source of happiness, make shared fun and enjoyment a priority.

Children – skills for a happy life

The secret of happy children, said Steve Biddulph (who wrote a book of the same title) is to love them unconditionally and to listen. And when asked what they want for their children, most parents will say, 'For them to be happy,' above all else.

As parents, we bring to this goal all sorts of preconceived ideas, past experiences and assumptions about what it means for a child to be happy and how it should be done or might be achieved. And sometimes, despite our best intentions, the actual happiness of our children can be in danger of being sacrificed to the goal of being a good parent.

Children are the hands by which we take hold of heaven.
Henry Ward Beecher

First things first

One of the first jobs of any parent is to create a secure environment in which a child can grow up happily. This is greatly enabled by ensuring a child gets enough sleep and regular meals because, as is abundantly clear to all parents, a tired, hungry child finds life difficult to cope with and will inevitably make those feelings felt, long before he or she can articulate anything else. In fact, the same applies to any of us; although, as adults, we're expected not to inflict our tired, hungry and grumpy behaviour on anyone else!

Be happy yourself

Happy parents tend to create a happy environment and this is picked up on by children as a normal way to be. Family life, especially with young children, can be hectic and very tiring. Don't aim for perfection, which can cripple you, but, as child psychologist Donald Winnicott says, aim for being a 'good enough' parent.

In the happiest of our childhood memories, our parents were happy too.

ROBERT BRAULT

Love unconditionally

Children, being children, will inevitably mess up along the way. That's part of how they learn, as we did before them. No child is intrinsically bad and 'bad' behaviour is often an effort to convey something that's difficult to express. Helping children understand cause and effect, and taking responsibility for themselves, happens gradually over time. So although we might not always like what our children say or do, they should never be made to feel that they are unloved or unlovable.

Relationships

The first secure relationship that a child has is with its primary caregiver and it is here that he or she will learn how to love and trust. If this first experience was secure, where all basic needs were lovingly met, creating a safe place to learn about the outside world, then from this first happy base a child can grow and develop good relationships of his or her own, moving from the family into the outside world.

> **It is easier to build strong children than to repair broken men.** *Frederick Douglass*

Unstructured play

Constantly organising a child doesn't allow them space for imaginative play, or learning how to find ways to amuse themselves without constant attention or interference. Give them the tools – an idea, some building bricks, a pen and paper, a book – and allow them space to get on with it. Balance any time spent on technology (an iPad, the television, a games console) with other options that allow the possibility for interaction with others – talking and listening, sharing and taking turns.

Making mistakes

Childhood is mostly a state of trial and error, and allowing kids to try for themselves and make their own mistakes (within the bounds of safety) helps them learn to trust their own capability and judgement which will, in turn, help them to manage whatever comes along later in life.

Never help a child with a task at which he feels he can succeed.

MARIA MONTESSORI

Exercise

Along with consistent sleep and regular meals, exercise is a positive use of physical energy and it's a good habit to get into for life. Walk when you can with young children, run around outside in the fresh air, suggest they join a football team; anything that fosters physical activity will pay dividends now and later, in terms of keeping physically fit and lifting the mood.

Deferred gratification

Learning how to take turns, wait for – and anticipate – treats and how to work towards a goal are all healthy approaches to the sort of challenges that arise in life. Learning patience and avoiding the sort of frustration that sits alongside impatience is a happier place to be.

We find delight in the beauty and happiness of children that makes the heart too big for the body. *Ralph Waldo Emerson*

Growing up happy

However good our childhood, however well-intentioned our parents, teachers and caregivers, growing up is not always a happy experience. It is also, inevitably, a time of growing awareness of our feelings, and this includes not only what makes us happy but also what doesn't.

Growing up is about exploring the ideas, values and attitudes we've been taught and making them our own, keeping some and discarding others. It's about finding out what works for you and what sort of person you want to be. In short, it's the beginning of taking ownership for what makes you happy and how you want to live your life. And that's not always an easy path to negotiate.

It takes courage to grow up and become who you really are.
e. e. cummings

Ask for help

You've no doubt heard those old proverbs, *'A problem shared is a problem halved'* and, *'Two heads are better than one'*. Sometimes it pays to ask for help, or share an experience, in order to get the support you need. Sometimes, just talking through a concern with a trusted friend or counsellor is a relief and can restore perspective and happiness. Keeping worries bottled up seldom improves things. And, sometimes, professional help (see pages 127–9) can make all the difference.

In 2015, the UK charity ChildLine (which works in association with the National Society for the Prevention of Cruelty to Children) said that family relationships, confidence and unhappiness were the biggest issues for young people. A total of 35,244 counselling sessions provided by ChildLine in 2014/15 were related to low self-esteem and unhappiness, a figure that was, sadly, up by 9 per cent on the previous year. **www.nspcc.org.uk**

Avoid comparisons

Wherever you look, there will always be those who appear to be more successful, better-looking or happier than you are. People's lives, from the outside, can look great even when the reality of their experience can be very different from what you see. Constantly comparing yourself to other people is unhelpful: there will always be those who are better or worse off than you are.

Facebook

One of the worst places for making comparisons is on social media. This applies to Facebook in particular, where every photo and status post can be edited and manipulated. The number of 'Likes' someone receives can look like a statement of popularity and success, and the reverse seems true if there are none. However much anyone tells you that Facebook and other social media (Instagram, Twitter) is not the real world, it can seem very seductive. Treat it with caution and give it a wide berth if it makes you unhappy in any way.

We live in a time when high self-esteem is encouraged from childhood, when young people have more freedom and independence than ever, but also far more depression, anxiety, cynicism and loneliness... More than any other generation in history, the children of Baby Boomers are disappointed by what they find when they arrive at adulthood.

DR JEAN TWENGE, AUTHOR OF *GENERATION ME*

Unrealistic expectations

Sometimes, in a hurry to grow up, we can harbour unrealistic expectations of the lives we lead – or think we should be leading. Feeling confident about our capabilities is one thing but it can sometimes mask the quite natural uncertainty that is part and parcel of growing up. The idea that we can achieve without hard work is everywhere, and fostered by the very unreal idea of overnight celebrity status. But the reality is that for most 'overnight sensations' it has usually taken years and years to get there, with setbacks, failures and disappointments along the way, as well as all the fun that can come from trying. So it's as well to be realistic and look at what it takes and to ensure that the journey along the way is a good one, too.

I have missed more than 9,000 shots in my career. I have lost almost 300 games. On 26 occasions I have been entrusted to take the game-winning shot... and I missed. I have failed over and over and over again in my life. And that's precisely why I succeed.

MICHAEL JORDAN, GREATEST BASKETBALL PLAYER OF ALL TIME

Growing old happy

If we are fortunate, we live long enough to grow old. If we are doubly fortunate, we live well enough to enjoy growing old. But, like so much else about being happy, this depends in part on our attitude. And our attitude towards ageing could be what makes all the difference to whether or not it's a happy experience.

> **He who is of a calm and happy nature will hardly feel the pressure of age, but to him who is of an opposite disposition, youth and age are equally a burden.** *Plato*

When does growing old start?

Is this when we physically age, or when we age mentally? Does it happen at 45 or at 85 years of age? The jury is out on this, but as far as we are individually concerned, an element of choice remains – and choosing to take those steps that support an active and happy life are pretty much the same as at any other time of life.

At the end of the 19th century, the average life expectancy was around 40 years old. Today, it's double that and so it's worth planning how to make the best use of this extra time. Firstly, reject those horrible stereotypes of age – don't become a grumpy old man or woman. Savour the positives and seek out new pleasures, while expressing gratitude for the joy already in your life.

> **You don't stop laughing when you grow old; you grow old when you stop laughing.** *George Bernard Shaw*

Stay strong

Inevitably there's a degree of physical deterioration as we age, and this comes down partly to our genes (for example, we may have a genetic predisposition towards osteoarthritis) but we can support our physical health and reduce our risk of age-related illnesses by keeping active. Regular exercise to support physical and mental health is important throughout our lives (see pages 65–71), so finding suitable ways to continue to exercise as we age is key.

Muscle tone can be improved at any age – so it's never, ever too late to start or resume regular exercise – and this goes a long way to supporting our bones, ligaments, tendons and internal organs, reducing pain and keeping our posture strong.

Exercising our muscles also produces what John Ratey, author of *Spark: The Revolutionary New Science of Exercise and the Brain*, calls 'Miracle-Gro' for the brain. BDNF, or brain-derived neurotropic factor, helps build neurotransmitters and their connections in the brain, along with mood-enhancing dopamine and serotonin. When we exercise, our muscles produce a protein called IGF-1 (insulin-like growth factor 1), which stimulates the production of BDNF in the brain. So, while keeping your body strong, the brain's function is also stimulated: a win-win.

Take your pick – yoga for focus, flexibility and muscle strength; Pilates for core stability; walking for weight-bearing and bone density; cycling for muscle tone and balance; any exercise for companionship and fun!

Breath is the power behind all things. Your breath doesn't know how old you are; it doesn't know what you can't do. If I'm feeling puzzled or my mind is telling me that I'm not capable of something, I breathe in and know that good things will happen.

TAO PORCHON-LYNCH, YOGA INSTRUCTOR, AGE 94

Eat well

As we age, we need fewer calories to maintain a healthy body weight, but we still need great nutrients to keep functioning well: lots of good-quality protein from animal and vegetable sources, vitamins and minerals from a variety of fruit and vegetables every day, plus a little of what you fancy – in moderation, both dark chocolate and red wine have their benefits, too.

Stay curious

There has never been a better time to be curious, with a world at our fingertips – literally – from online resources. At any time, you can enjoy a TED lecture (www.ted.com) or access new music, online learning or online fun; not to mention the social networking that allows you to stay connected and have a chat with family and friends around the world.

Extend this curiosity beyond your screen and you have the potential to find happiness everywhere – while also keeping your mind stimulated, active and engaged; from a conversation with someone in the supermarket queue to the ingredients for a new dish you want to try on its shelves, from the evening class you sign up for to the trip abroad you take.

Curiosity can broaden our minds, both factually and philosophically. It can keep us in touch with the world around us, and make us more mindful of it while also enriching our lives and relationships, whatever our age.

> **At age 20, we worry about what others think of us. At age 40, we don't care what they think of us. At age 60, we discover they haven't been thinking of us at all.**
> *Ann Landers*

Stay connected

All research-based evidence about happiness shows that it's having good personal relationships, with partners, family and friends, that helps support our happiness. As we age, we can lose those we love and feelings of isolation and loneliness can creep in. Guard against this, be open to new friendships and possibilities, create opportunities to mix with and meet people, those you know and those you've not yet met. Prioritise those you love but maintain other social networks. And be open to all age groups; everyone has something to offer.

Count your age by friends, not years. Count your life by smiles, not tears.

JOHN LENNON

Positive steps that can help

To be happy 100 per cent of the time isn't possible. Feeling happy sits alongside other feelings, like frustration, anger, sadness and sometimes despair. It is, however, our ability to manage unhappy times that relies, in part, on our overall approach to life, our health, our relationships, and the support we seek and receive when we need it. If we are resilient, of an optimistic nature, given to seeing the positive in life and having a sense of perspective about it, we tend to manage unhappy times better, knowing they will pass.

Have a strategy for the down times

However happy our lives, we all need a strategy for when life throws a curveball our way. Feeling mildly depressed or unhappy about something specific can be an entirely relevant or reasonable response to life and we need to know that it will usually pass in its own time, and there are things we can do to help ourselves through it. This is sometimes referred to as a reactive or temporary depression, and self-help treatment (as suggested below) can be very effective in restoring our happiness.

Touch is as essential as sunlight.

DIANE ACKERMAN

THE HAPPINESS CHALLENGE
- **Be mindful**: do less and notice more
- **Be kind**: do things for others
- **Be grateful**: remember the good things

(SOURCE: ACTION FOR HAPPINESS, WWW.ACTIONFORHAPPINESS.ORG)

Take care of yourself

When everything else is going haywire – for example, if you're in a state of grief – don't neglect your physical health. Get enough sleep, eat healthily, take regular exercise, even if it's only a daily walk to help lift your mood. It may not seem to help, but it will pay off in the longer term. If you are struggling with any of this – for example, chronic insomnia or loss of appetite – seek professional help. If you can avoid physical fallout at this stage, it will help you get back to feeling happier, faster.

Also avoid any reliance on alcohol, recreational or other drugs (unless specifically prescribed by your doctor), or even excessive caffeinated drinks, that will affect your sleep, make you jittery and your life more difficult to manage. Getting overtired can be debilitating to your mood, making everything worse, so do everything you can to keep sleeping well.

Confide in friends

Allow friends to support you. Sometimes it's helpful to confide in just one or two friends, who know you well and are not judgemental, about what you are going through rather than broadcast it to each and every one. Sometimes you might need to just spend time doing something together with a friend – taking a walk, going to a movie, seeing an exhibition – that is undemanding, but distracts and refocuses your perspective. Just the physical proximity of a friend can be consoling; a hug can be hugely comforting.

Be active

Managing some routine – getting up in the morning, walking to the local shop and reconnecting with the outside world, getting some fresh air and sunlight – can help shift negative moods. Exercise actually lifts the mood (see page 65) so if possible try to do a little exercise every day – it will help keep your sleep pattern regular, too. Set yourself a daily goal – making your bed, going to work, cooking a meal – something that helps you maintain a sense of order and the feeling that you're staying on top of things.

Just keep going. No feeling is final. *Rainer Maria Rilke*

Be kind to yourself

Do what you would for a friend who was feeling low. Think about what might be nice – a relaxing bath, a bunch of flowers, watching a movie with friends, a soothing massage – any small treat that distracts and relaxes you and takes your mind off the negative for a while.

Time

Give yourself time. It may be a cliché to say it, but it is a great healer. If you've had a bereavement, or experienced the end of an important relationship, or a prolonged period of stress, it takes time to recalibrate

One of the secrets of a happy life is continuous small treats.

IRIS MURDOCH

psychologically and physically, and often much longer than people think it will. Some traumas are very difficult to deal with: you never get over the death of a child, for example, but you do learn to live with it and most find happiness again. But it takes time. Grief isn't something that ends, but it's a process and does change and, a bit like convalescence, it pays to be as gentle and kind to yourself as you would be to others during this process.

Seek help

If your feelings of sadness or unhappiness continue for a long period of time, or if you feel you are not managing very well and could benefit from some professional support, see your doctor for help, advice and a possible referral for expert help (see pages 127–9).

Additional help to be happy – when it's needed & how to get it

Talking treatments

Your doctor or physician should be able to suggest what might be suitable or advisable for you, and what may be available to you in your area. In many cases, once you have an idea of what might be most helpful, you can self-refer. Whatever you decide, it's worth considering a) what you would like it to achieve and b) the approach and training of any therapist or counsellor you work with. It's also important that any therapist consulted is properly trained, supervised and abides by an acceptable standard of professional ethics. Most are accredited to a professional body – for example, in the UK the British Association for Counselling and Psychotherapy is a professional body to which registered therapists are accountable.

Happiness does not depend on outward things, but on the way we see them. *Leo Tolstoy*

› *Cognitive behavioural therapy (CBT)*

This helps to identify and change those negative thoughts that contribute to feeling anxious and depressed. For mild depression, online CBT might be offered, either for use alone or in addition to sessions with a CBT-trained therapist.

› *Mindfulness-based cognitive therapy (MBCT)*

This approach focuses on being mindful, by consistently paying attention to the present moment and viewing life in a non-judgemental way, rather than persistently going over and over worries. In addition, MBCT can form the basis of group therapy.

› *Counselling*

This involves talking with someone who is trained to listen with empathy and acceptance. It allows you to express your feelings and helps you to find your own solutions to your problems.

› *Psychotherapy*

With a focus on past experiences and how these may be contributing to experiences and feelings in the present, psychotherapy can be short or long term. In addition, it may be more frequent and intensive than counselling, and may go deeply into childhood experience and significant relationships.

› *Group therapy*

Run by a trained therapist, this allows a group of people to work together and support each other in facing and tackling their problems. Some people find it easier to talk with others who have similar experiences, and find their shared insights helpful.

Medication

In some cases, either in the short or long term, medication can be very helpful for depression that is more than mild. The most commonly used antidepressants are those of the SSRI (selective serotonin reuptake inhibitors) variety, which are prescribed under a number of different names, including Prozac, Cipramil, Seroxat and Lustral. These antidepressants are usually well tolerated but for many it takes up to four weeks for them to have an actual effect on symptoms of depression. It also takes time to adjust to some of the common side effects, but this is very individual. Medication can be helpful in resolving initial symptoms of depression and anxiety, and can also be useful in conjunction with talking therapies.

Self-help

Whatever the causes of unhappiness, depression or other mental health issues, the self-help measures outlined in this book should also be used. Whatever your situation, paying attention to your physical health will support your mental health. Good nutrition, regular exercise, adequate downtime and good sleep habits are important for everyone.

Self-knowledge is no guarantee of happiness but it is on the side of happiness and can supply the courage to fight for it.

SIMONE DE BEAUVOIR

We either make ourselves happy or miserable.

The amount of work is the same.

CARLOS CASTANEDA

CONCLUSION

Choosing happiness

Is it possible to make a conscious choice to be happy?

Ever since happiness heard your name, it has been running through the streets trying to find you. *Hafiz*

Happiness is not just one state of mind but can vary from day to day, hour to hour, even minute to minute, and is often influenced by things outside our control. The trick is to maintain perspective, not to base your happiness on things outside your control and not to let anything someone else has said or done derail you.

The many faces of happiness

What does it mean to you to be happy? Is it the feeling of peaceful satisfaction you get when a job's well done? Is it the joy you feel watching your beloved dog run for a ball? Or your toddler's delight at jumping in a muddy puddle? Is it that feeling of contentment with yourself as you appreciate a beautiful sky, or the euphoria felt from singing Handel's 'Hallelujah Chorus' in a choir?

Be happy for this moment. This moment is your life.

Omar Khayyam

Start now

Happiness can sometimes feel very elusive. There will always be times when we feel tired, depressed or sad, and this is normal. But if there are aspects of our lives that can be improved, often through quite simple means, and these improvements will make a difference to your happiness, then it's worth considering, isn't it? You might feel that it's those things outside your control that are marring your happiness. But there's always a difference that can be made – even if it's just a choice about not sweating the small stuff, investing more in a relationship, or saying no to a demand that doesn't serve your greater wellbeing. Don't put your life or your happiness on hold: start now to make a difference.

In her book *The How of Happiness*, professor of psychology Sonja Lyubomirsky concludes that 50 per cent of our happiness level is genetically determined (based on twin studies), 10 per cent is affected by life circumstances and situation, but the remaining 40 per cent is subject to how we choose to be. Given that this shows it's perfectly possible to actively choose a substantial degree of happiness, why wouldn't you?

Dr Martin Seligman identified three kinds of happiness: the pleasant life, the good life and the meaningful life, suggesting that there needs to

10%
HAPPINESS AFFECTED BY
OUTSIDE INFLUENCES

50%
GENETICALLY
DETERMINED
HAPPINESS

40%
HOW HAPPY WE
CHOOSE TO BE

be a balance between all three for a happy life. What is useful perhaps is
to look at how these three aspects might play out in your own life – and
where steps might need to be taken to improve and sustain your own
happiness. It might be that life is very meaningful, but not much fun;
or that you are lonely and missing those with whom to share more. By
choosing, say, to include more connection or relaxation or fun in life,
to complement its other aspects, you could make a big difference to
your happiness. And, in this way, you are actively choosing to create the
possibility for your own happiness.

Rules for happiness: something to do, someone to love, something to hope for.

IMMANUEL KANT

Acknowledgements

In the writing of this book, I'd like to acknowledge all my friends and professional colleagues for those insights and wisdom that have contributed and, in particular, Susan Clark. I'm also grateful for the continued support of my publisher, in particular Kate Pollard, Kajal Mistry and Hannah Roberts. Working with the team at Hardie Grant continues to be a happy experience – thank you! Thanks are also due to Julia Murray, whose talent for illustration and design ensures my words are brought to life.

I would also like to thank my sons, Josh and Robbie, for the happy contribution they continue to make to my life, and in the hope that their own paths in life continue to be happy ones.

Appendix

Further reading

Happiness – Essential Mindfulness Practices,
Thich Nhat Hanh (Parallax Press, 2009)

Learned Optimism,
Martin Seligman, PhD (Vintage Books USA, 2006)

The Art of Happiness,
The Dalai Lama & Howard Cutler (Hodder Paperbacks, 1999)

The How of Happiness,
Sonja Lyubomirsky (Piatkus Books, 2010)

Useful websites

www.actionforhappiness.org

www.headspace.com

www.itsgoodtotalk.org.uk

www.mind.org.uk

About the author

Harriet Griffey is a journalist, writer and author of numerous books focused on health. Along with *I want to be happy*, she is the author of four other books in this series: *I want to sleep*, *I want to be calm*, *I want to be organised* and *I want to be confident*, all published by Hardie Grant. Other published books include *The Art of Concentration* (Rodale, 2010), *How to Get Pregnant* (Bloomsbury Publishing, 2010), and *Give Your Child a Better Start* (with Professor Mike Howe; Penguin Books, 1995). She originally trained as a nurse, writes and broadcasts regularly on health and health-related issues, and is also an accredited coach with Youth at Risk (www.youthatrisk.org.uk).

Harriet

Index

I want to be happy by Harriet Griffey

First published in 2017 by Hardie Grant Books

Hardie Grant Books (UK)
52–54 Southwark Street
London SE1 1UN
hardiegrant.co.uk

Hardie Grant Books (Australia)
Ground Floor, Building 1
658 Church Street
Melbourne, VIC 3121
hardiegrant.com.au

The moral rights of Harriet Griffey to be identified as the author
of this work have been asserted by her in accordance with the
Copyright, Designs and Patents Act 1988.

Text © Harriet Griffey
Illustrations © Julia Murray

All rights reserved. No part of this publication may be reproduced,
stored in a retrieval system or transmitted in any form by any
means, electronic, electrostatic, magnetic tape, mechanical,
photocopying, recording or otherwise, without
the prior written permission of the Publisher.

British Library Cataloguing-in-Publication Data. A catalogue record
for this book is available from the British Library.

ISBN: 978-1-78488-080-4

Publisher: Kate Pollard
Senior Editor: Kajal Mistry
Editorial Assistant: Hannah Roberts
Internal and Cover Design: Julia Murray
Internal and Cover Illustrations: Julia Murray
Copy Editor: Charlotte Coleman-Smith
Proofreader: Clare Hubbard
Indexer: Cathy Heath
Colour Reproduction by p2d

Printed and bound in China by 1010

10 9 8 7 6 5 4 3 2 1